cover of the 1870 edition from
Cameron and Ferguson,
London, Glasgow.

MOCHA DICK
OR THE
WHITE WHALE OF THE PACIFIC
BY. J.N.REYNOLDS.

CAMERON & FERGUSON
LONDON & GLASGOW

Mocha Dick:

or the White Whale
of the Pacific:
A Leaf from a Manuscript Journal

by
J. N. Reynolds

SicPress 2013
Methuen, Mass.

"Mocha Dick: or the White Whale of the Pacific: A Leaf from a Manuscript Journal" was originally published in *The Knickerbocker, or New-York Monthly Magazine* in May 1839, it was reprinted alone in 1870 by Cameron and Ferguson of London and Glasgow, and again in 1932 by Charles Scribner's and Sons, New York.

©2013

SicPress.com

14 Pleasant St.

Methuen, Massachusetts.

sales@sicpress.com

INTRODUCTION

Jeremiah N. Reynolds (1799–1858), was an American newspaper editor, lecturer, explorer and author who became an influential advocate for scientific expeditions. His lectures on the possibility of a hollow earth appear to have influenced Edgar Allan Poe's *The Narrative of Arthur Gordon Pym of Nantucket* (1838) and his 1839 account of the whale Mocha Dick, "Mocha Dick: Or the White Whale of the Pacific", influenced Herman Melville's *Moby-Dick* (1851).

Born into poverty in Pennsylvania, he moved to Ohio as a child. In his teenage years and early 20s, he taught school, saved his money and attended Ohio University in Athens, Ohio for three years. He then edited *the Spectator* newspaper in Wilmington, Ohio, but sold his interest in it in about 1823.

The next year, Reynolds began a lecture tour with John Cleves Symmes, Jr.. Reynolds had become a convert to Symmes' theory that the earth is hollow. Symmes' idea was accepted as possible by some respected scientists of the time. The two presented talks on the subject. When Symmes died, Reynolds continued his lectures, which were given to full houses in Eastern U.S. cities (with a charge of 50 cents for admission). Over time, Reynolds became willing to accept the possibility that the theory was wrong. In Philadelphia, Reynolds and Symmes parted.

Gaining the support of members of President John Quincy Adams' cabinet, and speaking before Congress, Reynolds succeeded in fitting out a national expedition to the South Pole. But Andrew Jackson opposed the project, and after he became president it was squelched. Reynolds garnered support from private sources and the expedition sailed from New York City in 1829. With much danger, the expedition reached the Antarctic shore and returned north, but at Valparaíso, Chile, the crew mutinied and set Reynolds and another man on shore.

In 1832, the United States frigate "Potomac" under Commodore John Downes arrived. The ship had been ordered to the coast of Sumatra to avenge an attack on an American ship, "Friendship", of Salem, Massachusetts and was returning home in what became a circumnavigation of the globe. Reynolds joined Downes as his private secretary for the trip and in 1835 he wrote a book about the experience, *Voyage of the United States frigate Potomac : under the command of Commodore John Downes, during the circum-navigation of the globe, in the years 1831, 1832, 1833, and 1834.*

Reynolds gathered first-hand observations of Mocha Dick, an albino sperm whale off Chile who bedeviled a generation of whalers for thirty years before succumbing to one. Mocha Dick survived many skirmishes (by some accounts at least 100) with whalers before he was eventually killed. He was large and powerful, capable of wrecking small craft with his flukes. In May 1839, *The Knickerbocker, or New-York Monthly Magazine* published Reynolds' "Mocha Dick: Or the White Whale of the Pacific," the inspiration for Herman Melville's 1851 novel *Moby-Dick.*

According to Reynolds, the whale's head was covered with barnacles, which gave him a rugged appearance. The whale also had a peculiar method of spouting: "Instead of projecting his spout obliquely forward, and puffing with a short, convulsive effort, accompanied by a snorting noise, as usual with his species, he flung the water from his nose in a lofty, perpendicular, expanded volume, at regular and somewhat distant intervals; its expulsion producing a continuous roar, like that of vapor struggling from the safety valve of a powerful steam engine."

Mocha Dick was most likely first encountered and attacked sometime prior to the year 1810 off Mocha Island. His survival of the first encounters coupled with his unusual appearance quickly made him famous among Nantucket whalers. Many captains attempted to hunt him after rounding Cape Horn. He was quite docile, sometimes swimming alongside the ship, but once attacked he retaliated with ferocity and cunning, and was widely feared by harpooners. When agitated he would sound and then breach so aggressively that his entire body would sometimes come completely out of the water. In Reynolds' account, Mocha Dick was killed in 1838, after he appeared to come to the aid of a distraught cow whose calf had just been slain by the whalers. His body was 70 feet long and yielded 100 barrels of oil, along with some ambergris. He also had several harpoons in his body.

In 1841, Harper Bros, published Reynolds' *Address on the subject of a surveying and exploring expedition to the Pacific Ocean and South Seas: Delivered in the Hall of Representatives on the evening of April 3, 1836.*

Reynolds studied law and became a success as an advocate in New York City. In 1848, he organized a stock company in New York City for a New Mexico mining operation. Reynolds missed joining the Great U.S. Exploring Expedition of 1838-1842, even though that venture was a result of his agitation. He did not participate because he had offended too many in his call for such a trip. His health broke down and in 1858 he died in New York at age 59.

MOCHA DICK:

OR THE WHITE WHALE OF THE PACIFIC: A LEAF FROM A MANUSCRIPT JOURNAL

We expected to find the island of Santa Maria still more remarkable for the luxuriance of its vegetation, than even the fertile soil of Mocha; and the disappointment arising from the unexpected shortness of our stay at the latter place, was in some degree relieved, by the prospect of our remaining for several days in safe anchorage at the former. Mocha lies upon the coast of Chili, in lat. 38" 28' south, twenty leagues north of Mono del Bonifacio, and opposite the Imperial river, from which it bears w. s. w. During the last century, this island was inhabited by the Spaniards, but it is at present, and has been for some years, entirely deserted. Its climate is mild, with little perceptible difference of temperature between the summer and winter seasons. Frost is unknown on the lowlands, and snow is rarely seen, even on the summits of the loftiest mountains.

It was late in the afternoon, when we left the schooner; and while we bore up for the north, she stood away for the southern extremity of the island. As evening was gathering around us, we fell in with a vessel, which proved to be the same whose boats, a day or two before, we had seen in the act of taking a whale. Aside from the romantic and stirring associations it awakened, there are few objects in themselves

9

more picturesque or beautiful, than a whaleship, seen from a distance of three or four miles, on a pleasant evening, in the midst of the great Pacific. As she moves gracefully over the water, rising and falling on the gentle undulations peculiar to this sea; her sails glowing in the quivering light of the fires that flash from below, and a thick volume of smoke ascending from the midst, and curling away in dark masses upon the wind; it requires little effort of the fancy, to imagine one's self gazing upon a floating volcano.

As we were both standing to the north, under easy sail, at nine o'clock at night we had joined company with the stranger. Soon after, we were boarded by his whale-boat, the officer in command of which bore us the compliments of the captain, together with a friendly invitation to partake the hospitalities of his cabin. Accepting, without hesitation, a courtesy so frankly tendered, we proceeded, in company with Captain Palmer, on board, attended by the mate of *the Penguin*, who was on his way to St. Mary's to repair his boat, which had some weeks before been materially injured in a storm.

We found the whaler a large, well-appointed ship, owned in New-York, and commanded by such a man as one might expect to find in charge of a vessel of this character; plain, unassuming, intelligent, and well-informed upon all the subjects relating to his peculiar calling. But what shall we say of his first mate, or how describe him? To attempt his portrait by a comparison, would be vain, for we have never looked upon his like, and a detailed description, however accurate, would but faintly shadow forth the tout ensemble of his extraordinary figure. He had probably numbered about thirty-five years. We arrived at this conclusion, however, rather from the untamed brightness of his flashing eye, than the general appearance of his features, on which torrid sun and polar storm had left at once the furrows of more advanced age, and a tint swarthy as that of the Indian. His height, which was a little beneath the common standard, appeared almost dwarfish, from the immense breadth of his overhanging shoulders, while the unnatural length of the loose, dangling arms which hung from them, and which, when at rest, had least the appearance of ease, imparted to his uncouth and muscular frame an air of grotesque awkwardness, which defies description. He made few pretensions as a sailor, and had never aspired to the command of a ship. But he would not have exchanged the sensations which stirred his blood, when steering down upon a school of whales, for the privilege of treading, as master, the deck of the noblest liner that ever traversed the Atlantic. According to the admeasurement of his philosophy, whaling was the most dignified and manly of all sublunary pursuits. Of this he felt perfectly satisfied, having been engaged in the noble vocation for upward of twenty years, during which period, if his own assertions were to be received as evidence, no man in the American spermaceti fleet had made so many captures, or met with such wild adventures, in the exercise of his perilous profession. Indeed, so completely were all his propensities, thoughts, and feelings, identified with his occupation; so intimately did he seem acquainted with the habits and instincts of the objects of his pursuit, and so little conversant with the ordinary affairs of life; that one felt less inclined to class him in the genus homo, than as a sort of intermediate something between man and the cetaceous tribe.

Soon after the commencement of his nautical career, in order to prove that he was not afraid of a whale, a point which it is essential for the young whaleman to establish beyond question, he offered, upon a wager, to run his boat "bows on" against the side of an "old bull", leap from the "cuddy" to the back of the fish, sheet his lance home, and return on board in safety. This feat, daring as it may be considered, he undertook and accomplished; at least so it was chronicled in his log, and he was ready to bear witness, on oath, to the veracity of the record. But his conquest of the

11

redoubtable Mocha Dick, unquestionably formed the climax of his exploits.

Before we enter into the particulars of this triumph, which, through their valorous representative, conferred so much honor on the lancers of Nantucket, it may be proper to inform the reader who and what Mocha Dick was; and thus give him a posthumous introduction to one who was, in his day and generation, so emphatically among fish the "Stout Gentleman" of his latitudes. The introductory portion of his history we shall give, in a condensed form, from the relation of the mate. Substantially, however, it will be even as he rendered it; and as his subsequent narrative, though not deficient in rude eloquence, was coarse in style and language, as well as unnecessarily diffuse, we shall assume the liberty of altering the expression; of adapting the phraseology to the occasion; and of presenting the whole matter in a shape more succinct and connected. In this arrangement, however, we shall leave our adventurer to tell his own story, although not always in his own words, and shall preserve the person of the original.

But to return to Mocha Dick — which, it may be observed, few were solicitous to do, who had once escaped from him. This renowned monster, who had come off victorious in a hundred fights with his pursuers, was an old bull whale, of prodigious size and strength. From the effect of age, or more probably from a freak of nature, as exhibited in the case of the Ethiopian Albino, a singular consequence had resulted — he was white as wool! Instead of projecting his spout obliquely forward, and puffing with a short, convulsive effort, accompanied by a snorting noise, as usual with his species, he flung the water from his nose in a lofty, perpendicular, expanded volume, at regular and somewhat distant intervals; its expulsion producing a continuous roar, like that of vapor struggling from the safety-valve of a powerful steam engine. Viewed from a distance, the practised eye of the sailor only could decide, that the moving mass, which constituted this enormous animal, was not a white cloud sailing along the horizon. On the spermaceti whale, barnacles are rarely discovered; but upon the head of this lusus naturae, they had clustered, until it became absolutely rugged with the shells. In short, regard him as you would, he was a most extraordinary fish; or, in the vernacular of Nantucket, "a genuine old sog", of the first water.

Opinions differ as to the time of his discovery. It is settled, however, that previous to the year 1810, he had been seen and attacked near the island of Mocha. Numerous boats are known to have been shattered by his immense flukes, or ground to pieces in the crush of his powerful jaws; and, on one occasion, it is said that he came off victorious from a conflict with the crews of three English whalers, striking fiercely at the last of the retreating boats, at the moment it was rising from the water, in its hoist up to the ship's davits. It must not be supposed, howbeit, that through all this desperate warfare, our leviathan passed scathless. A back serried with irons, and from fifty to a hundred yards of line trailing in his wake, sufficiently attested, that though unconquered, he had not proved invulnerable. From the period of Dick's first appearance, his celebrity continued to increase, until his name seemed naturally to mingle with the salutations which whalemen were in the habit of exchanging, in their encounters upon the broad Pacific; the customary interrogatories almost always closing with, "Any news from Mocha Dick?" Indeed, nearly every whaling captain who rounded Cape Horn, if he possessed any professional ambition, or valued himself on his skill in subduing the monarch of the seas, would lay his vessel along the coast, in the hope of having an opportunity to try the muscle of this doughty champion, who was never known to shun his assailants. It was remarked, nevertheless, that the old fellow seemed particularly careful as to the portion of his body which he exposed to the approach of the boat-steerer; generally presenting, by some well-timed manoeuvre, his back to the harpooneer; and dexterously evading every attempt to plant an iron under his fin, or a spade on his "small". Though naturally fierce, it was not customary with Dick, while unmolested, to betray a malicious disposition. On the contrary, he would sometimes pass quietly round a vessel, and occasionally swim lazily and harmlessly among the boats, when armed with full craft, for the destruction of his race. But this forbearance gained him little credit, for if no other cause of accusation remained to them, his foes would swear they saw a lurking deviltry in the long, careless sweep of his flukes. Be this as it may, nothing is more certain, than that all indifference vanished with the first prick of the harpoon; while cutting the line, and a hasty retreat to their vessel, were frequently the only means of escape from destruction, left to his discomfited assaulters.

Thus far the whaleman had proceeded in his story and was about commencing the relation of his own individual encounters with its subject, when he was cut short by the mate of *the Penguin*, to whom allusion has already been made, and who had remained, up to this point, an excited and attentive listener. Thus he would have continued, doubtless, to the end of the chapter, notwithstanding his avowed contempt for every other occupation than sealing, had not an observation escaped the narrator, which tended to arouse his professional jealousy. The obnoxious expression we have forgotten. Probably it involved something of boasting or egotism; for no sooner was it uttered, than our sealer sprang from his seat, and planting himself in front of the unconscious author of the insult, exclaimed:

"You! — you whale-killing, blubber-hunting, light-gathering varmint! — you pretend to manage a boat better than a Stonington sealer! A Nantucket whaleman," he continued, curling his lip with a smile of supreme disdain, "presume to teach a Stonington sealer how to manage a boat! Let all the small craft of your South Sea fleet range among the rocks and breakers where I have been, and if the whales would not have a peaceful time of it, for the next few years, may I never strip another jacket, or book another skin! What's taking a whale? Why, I could reeve a line through one's blow-hole, make it fast to a thwart, and then beat his brains out with my seal-club!"

Having thus given play to the first ebullition of his choler, he proceeded with more calmness to institute a comparison between whaling and sealing. "A whaler," said he, "never approaches land, save when he enters a port to seek fresh grub. Not so the sealer. He thinks that his best fortune, which leads him where the form of man has never before startled the game he's after; where a quick eye, steady nerve, and stout heart, are his only guide and defence, in difficulty and danger. Where the sea is roughest, the whirlpool wildest, and the surf roars and dashes madly among the jagged cliffs, there — I was going to say there only — are the peak-nosed, black-eyed rogues we hunt for, to be found, gambolling in the white foam, and there must the sealer follow them. Were I to give you an account of my adventures about the Falkland Isles; off the East Keys of Staten Land; through the South Shetlands; off the Cape, where we lived on salt pork and seal's flippers; and finally, the story of a season spent with a single boat's crew on Diego Ramirez, you would not make such a fuss about your Mocha Dick. As to the straits of Magellen, Sir, they are as familiar to me, as Broadway to a New-York dandy; though it should strut along that fashionable promenade twelve dozen times a day."

Our son of the sea would have gone on to particularize his "hair-breadth 'scapes and moving accidents", had we not interposed, and insisted that the remainder of the night should be devoted to the conclusion of Dick's history; at the same time assuring the "knight of the club" that so soon as we met

15

at Santa Maria, he should have an entire evening expressly set apart, on which he might glorify himself and his calling. To this he assented, with the qualification, that his compliance with the general wish, in thus yielding precedence to his rival, should not be construed into an admission, that Nantucket whalemen were the best boatmen in the world, or that sealing was not as honorable and as pretty a business for coining a penny, as the profession of "blubber-hunting" ever was.

The whaler now resumed. "I will not weary you," said he, "with the uninteresting particulars of a voyage to Cape Horn. Our vessel, as capital a ship as ever left the little island of Nantucket, was finely manned and commanded, as well as thoroughly provided with every requisite for the peculiar service in which she was engaged. I may here observe, for the information of such among you as are not familiar with these things, that soon after a whale-ship from the United States is fairly at sea, the men are summoned aft; then boats' crews are selected by the captain and first mate, and a ship-keeper, at the same time, is usually chosen. The place to be filled by this individual is an important one and the person designated should be a careful and sagacious man. His duty is, more particularly, to superintend the vessel while the boats are away, in chase of fish; and at these times, the cook and steward are perhaps his only crew. His station, on these occasions, is at the mast-head, except when he is wanted below to assist in working the ship. While aloft, he is to look out for whales, and also to keep a strict and tireless eye upon the absentees, in order to render them immediate assistance, should emergency require it. Should the game rise to windward of their pursuers, and they be too distant to observe personal signs, he must run down the jib. If they rise to leeward he should haul up the spanker; continuing the little black signal-flag at the mast; so long as they remain on the surface. When the "school" turn flukes, and go down, the flag is to be struck, and again displayed when they are seen to ascend. When circumstances occur which require the return of the captain on board, the colors are to be hoisted at the mizzen peak. A ship-keeper must farther be sure that provisions are ready for the men, on their return from the chase, and that drink be amply furnished, in the form of a bucket of "switchel". "No whale, no switchel", is frequently the rule; but I am inclined to think that, whale or no whale, a little rum is not amiss, after a lusty pull.

"I have already said, that little of interest occurred, until after we had doubled Cape Horn. We were now standing in upon the coast of Chili, before a gentle breeze from the south, that bore us along almost imperceptibly. It was a quiet and beautiful evening, and the sea glanced and glistened in the level rays of the descending sun, with a surface of waving gold. The western sky was flooded with amber light, in the midst of which, like so many islands, floated immense clouds, of every conceivable brilliant dye; while far to the northeast, looming darkly against a paler heaven, rose the conical peak of Mocha. The men were busily employed in sharpening their harpoons, spades, and lances, for the expected fight. The look-out at the mast-head, with cheek on his shoulder, was dreaming of the "dangers he had passed", instead of keeping watch for those which were to come; while the captain paced the quarter-deck with long and hasty stride, scanning the ocean in every direction, with a keen, expectant eye. All at once, he stopped, fixed his gaze intently for an instant on some object to leeward, that seemed to attract it, and then, in no very conciliating tone, hailed the mast-head:

"'Both ports shut?' he exclaimed, looking aloft, and pointing backward, where a long white bushy spout was rising, about a mile off the larboard bow, against the glowing horizon. 'Both ports shut? I say, you leaden-eyed lubber! Nice lazy son of a sea-cook you are, for a look-out! Come down, Sir!'

"'There she blows! - sperm whale - old sog, sir,' said the man, in a deprecatory tone, as he descended from his nest in the air. It was at once seen that the creature was companionless; but as a lone whale is generally an old bull, and of unusual size and ferocity, more than ordinary sport was anticipated, while unquestionably more than ordinary honor was to be won from its successful issue.

"The second mate and I were ordered to make ready for pursuit; and now commenced a scene of emulation and excitement, of which the most vivid description would convey but an imperfect outline, unless you have been a spectator or an actor on a similar occasion. Line-tubs, water-kegs, and waif-poles, were thrown hurriedly into the boats; the irons were placed in the racks, and the necessary evolutions of the ship gone through, with a quickness almost magical; and this too, amidst what to a landsman would have seemed inextricable confusion, with perfect regularity and precision; the commands of the officers being all but forestalled by the enthusiastic eagerness of the men. In a short time, we were as near the object of our chase, as it was considered prudent to approach.

"'Back the main-top-s'l!' shouted the captain. 'There she blows! there she blows! — there she blows!' — cried the lookout, who had taken the place of his sleepy shipmate, raising the pitch of his voice with each announcement, until it amounted to a downright yell: 'Right ahead, Sir! — spout as long an 's thick as the mainyard!'

"'Stand by to lower!' exclaimed the captain; 'all hands; cook, steward, cooper — every d—d one of ye, stand by to lower!'

"An instantaneous rush from all quarters of the vessel answered this appeal, and every man was at his station, almost before the last word had passed the lips of the skipper.

"'Lower away!' — and in a moment the keels splashed in the water. 'Follow down the crews; jump in my boys; ship the crotch; line your oars; now pull, as if the d—l was in your wake!' were the successive orders, as the men slipped down the ship's side, took their places in the boats, and began to give way.

"The second mate had a little the advantage of me in starting. The stern of his boat grated against the bows of mine, at the instant I grasped my steering-oar, and gave the word to shove off. One sweep of my arm, and we sprang foaming in his track. Now came the tug of war. To become a first-rate oarsman, you must understand, requires a natural gift. My crew were not wanting in the proper qualification; every mother's son of them pulled as if he had been born with an oar in his hand; and as they stretched every sinew for the glory of darting the first iron it did my heart good to see the boys spring. At every stroke, the tough blades bent like willow wands, and quivered like tempered steel in the warm sunlight, as they sprang forward from the tension of the retreating wave. At the distance of half a mile and directly before us, lay the object of our emulation and ambition, heaving his huge bulk in unwieldy gambols, as though totally unconscious of our approach.

"'There he blows! An old bull, by Jupiter! Eighty barrels, boys, waiting to be towed alongside! Long and quick — shoot ahead! Now she feels it; waist boat never could beat us, now she feels the touch! — now she walks through it! Again — now!' Such were the broken exclamations and adjurations with which I cheered my rowers to their toil, as, with renewed vigor, I plied my long steering-oar. In another moment, we were alongside our competitor. The shivering blades flashed forward and backward, like sparks of light. The waters boiled under our prow, and the trenched waves closed, hissing and whirling, in our wake, as we swept, I might almost say were lifted, onward in our arrowy course.

"We were coming down upon our fish, and could hear the roar of his spouting above the rush of the sea, when my boat began to take the lead.

"'Now, my fine fellows,' I exclaimed, in triumph, 'now we'll show them our stern — only spring! Stand ready, harpooner, but don't dart, till I give the word.'

"'Carry me on, and his name's Dennis!' cried the boat-steerer, in a confident tone. We were perhaps a hundred feet in advance of the waist-boat, and within fifty of the whale, about an inch of whose hump only was to be seen above the water, when, heaving slowly into view a pair of flukes some eighteen feet in width, he went down. The men lay on their oars. 'There he blows, again!' cried the tub-oarsman, as a lofty, perpendicular spout sprang into the air, a few furlongs away on the starboard side. Presuming from his previous movement, that the old fellow had been 'gallied' by other boats, and might probably be jealous of our purpose, I was about ordering the men to pull away as softly and silently as possible, when we received fearful intimation that he had no intention of balking our inclination, or even yielding us the honor of the first attack. Lashing the sea with his enormous tail, until he threw about him a cloud of surf and spray, he came down, at full speed, 'jaws on', with the determination, apparently, of doing battle in earnest. As he drew near, with his long curved back looming occasionally above the surface of the billows, we perceived that it was white as the surf around him; and the men stared aghast at each other, as they uttered, in a suppressed tone, the terrible name of Mocha Dick!

"'Mocha Dick or the d—l,' said I, 'this boat never sheers off from any thing that wears the shape of a whale. Pull easy; just give her way enough to steer.' As the creature approached, he somewhat abated his frenzied speed, and, at the distance of a cable's length, changed his course to a sharp angle with our own.

"'Here he comes!' I exclaimed. 'Stand up, harpooner! Don't be hasty — don't be flurried. Hold your iron higher — firmer. Now!' I shouted, as I brought our bows within a boat's length of the immense mass which was wallowing heavily by. "Now! — give it to him solid!'

"But the leviathan plunged on, unharmed. The young harpooner, though ordinarily as fearless as a lion, had imbibed a sort of superstitious dread of Mocha Dick, from the exaggerated stories of that prodigy, which he had heard from his comrades. He regarded him, as he had heard him described in many a tough yarn during the middle watch, rather as some ferocious fiend of the deep, than a regular-built, legitimate whale! Judge then of his trepidation, on beholding a creature, answering the wildest dreams of his fancy, and sufficiently formidable, without any superadded terrors, bearing down upon him with thrashing flukes and distended jaws! He stood erect, it cannot be denied. He planted his foot — he grasped the coil — he poised his weapon. But his knee shook, and his sinewy arm wavered. The shaft was hurled, but with unsteady aim. It just grazed the back of the monster, glanced off, and darted into the sea beyond. A second, still more abortive, fell short of the mark. The giant animal swept on for a few rods, and then, as if in contempt of our fruitless and childish attempts to injure him, flapped a storm of spray in our faces with his broad tail, and dashed far down into the depths of the ocean, leaving our little skiff among the waters where he sank, to spin and duck in the whirlpool.

"Never shall I forget the choking sensation of disappointment which came over me at that moment. My glance fell on the harpooner. 'Clumsy lubber!' I vociferated, in a voice hoarse with passion; 'you a whaleman! You are only fit to spear eels! Cowardly spawn! Curse me, if you are not afraid of a whale!'

"The poor fellow, mortified at his failure, was slowly and thoughtfully hauling in his irons. No sooner had he heard me stigmatize him as 'afraid of a whale', than he bounded upon his thwart, as if bitten by a serpent. He stood before me for a moment, with a glowing cheek and flashing eye; then, dropping the iron he had just drawn in, without uttering a word, he turned half round, and sprang head-foremost into the sea. The tub-oarsman, who was recoiling the line in the after part of the boat, saw his design just in season to grasp him by the heel, as he made his spring. But he was not to be dragged on board again without a struggle. Having now become more calm, I endeavored to soothe his wounded pride with kind and flattering words; for I knew him to be a noble-hearted fellow, and was truly sorry that my hasty reproaches should have touched so fine a spirit so deeply.

"Night being now at hand, the captain's signal was set for our return to the vessel; and we were soon assembled on her deck, discussing the mischances of the day, and speculating on the prospect of better luck on the morrow.

"We were at breakfast next morning, when the watch at the fore-top-gallant head sung out merrily, 'There she breaches!' In an instant every one was on his feet. 'Where away?' cried the skipper, rushing from the cabin, and upsetting in his course the steward, who was returning from the caboose with a replenished biggin of hot coffee. 'Not loud but deep' were the grumblings and groans of that functionary, as he rubbed his scalded shins, and danced about in agony; but had they been far louder, they would have been drowned in the tumult of vociferation which answered the announcement from the mast-head.

"'Where away?' repeated the captain, as he gained the deck.

22

"'Three points off the leeward bow.'

"'How far?' "'About a league, Sir; heads same as we do. There she blows!' added the man, as he came slowly down the shrouds, with his eyes fixed intently upon the spouting herd.

"'Keep her off two points! Steady! — steady, as she goes!'

"'Steady it is, Sir,' answered the helmsman.

"'Weather braces, a small pull. Loose to'-gallant-s'ls! Bear a hand, my boys! Who knows but we may tickle their ribs at this rising?'

"The captain had gone aloft, and was giving these orders from the main-to'-gallant-cross-trees. 'There she top-tails! there she blows!' added he, as, after taking a long look at the sporting shoal, he glided down the back stay. 'Sperm whale, and a thundering big school of 'em!' was his reply to the rapid and eager inquiries of the men. 'See the lines in the boats,' he continued; 'get in the craft; swing the cranes!"

"By this time the fish had gone down, and every eye was strained to catch the first intimation of their reappearance. "'There she spouts!' screamed a young greenhorn in the main chains, 'close by; a mighty big whale, Sir!'

"'We'll know that better at the trying out, my son,' said the third mate, drily.

"'Back the main-top-s'l!' was now the command. The ship had little headway at the time, and in a few minutes we were as motionless as if lying at anchor.

"'Lower away, all hands!' And in a twinkling, and together, the starboard, larboard, and waist-boats struck the water. Each officer leaped into his own; the crews arranged themselves at their respective stations; the boat-steerers began to adjust their 'craft'; and we left the ship's side in company; the captain, in laconic phrase, bidding us to 'get up and get fast', as quickly as possible.

"Away we dashed, in the direction of our prey, who were frolicking, if such a term can be applied to their unwieldy motions, on the surface of the waves. Occasionally, a huge, shapeless body would flounce out of its proper element, and fall back with a heavy splash; the effort forming about as ludicrous a caricature of agility, as would the attempt of some over-fed alderman to execute the Highland fling.

"We were within a hundred rods of the herd, when, as if from a common impulse, or upon some preconcerted signal, they all suddenly disappeared. 'Follow me!' I shouted, waving my hand to the men in the other boats; 'I see their track under water; they swim fast, but we'll be among them when they rise. Lay back,' I continued, addressing myself to my own crew, 'back to the thwarts! Spring hard! We'll be in the thick of 'em when they come up; only pull!'

"And they did pull, manfully. After towing for about a mile, I ordered them to 'lie'. The oars were peaked, and we rose to look out for the first 'noddle-head' that should break water. It was at this time a dead calm. Not a single cloud was passing over the deep blue of the heavens, to vary their boundless transparency, or shadow for a moment the gleaming ocean which they spanned. Within a short distance lay our noble ship, with her idle canvass hanging in drooping festoons from her yards; while she seemed resting on her inverted image, which, distinct and beautiful as its original, was glassed in the smooth expanse beneath. No sound disturbed the general silence, save our own heavy breathings, the low gurgle of the water against the side of the boat, or the noise of flapping wings, as the albatross wheeled sleepily along through the stagnant atmosphere. We had remained quiet for about five minutes, when some dark object was descried ahead, moving on the surface of the sea. It proved to be a small 'calf', playing in the sunshine.

"'Pull up and strike it,' said I to the third mate; 'it may bring up the old one — perhaps the whole school.'

"And so it did, with a vengeance! The sucker was transpierced, after a short pursuit; but hardly had it made its first agonized plunge, when an enormous cow-whale rose close beside her wounded offspring. Her first endeavor was to take it under her fin, in order to bear it away; and nothing could be more striking than the maternal tenderness she manifested in her exertions to accomplish this object. But the poor thing was dying, and while she vainly tried to induce it to accompany her, it rolled over, and floated dead at her side. Perceiving it to be beyond the reach of her caresses, she turned to wreak her vengeance on its slayers, and made directly for the boat, crashing her vast jaws the while, in a paroxysm of rage. Ordering his boat-steerer aft, the mate sprang forward, cut the line loose from the calf, and then snatched from the crotch the remaining iron, which he plunged with his gathered strength into the body of the mother, as the boat sheered off to avoid her onset. I saw that the work was well done, but had no time to mark the issue; for at that instant, a whale 'breached' at the distance of about a mile from us, on the starboard quarter. The glimpse I caught of the animal in his descent, convinced me that I once more beheld my old acquaintance, Mocha Dick. That falling mass was white as a snow-drift!

"One might have supposed the recognition mutual, for no sooner was his vast square head lifted from the sea, than he charged down upon us, scattering the billows into spray as he advanced, and leaving a wake of foam a rod in width, from the violent lashing of his flukes.

"'He's making for the bloody water!' cried the men, as he cleft his way toward the very spot where the calf had been killed. 'Here, harpooner, steer the boat, and let me dart!' I exclaimed, as I leaped into the bows. 'May the 'Goneys' eat me, if he dodge us this time. though he were Beelzebub himself! Pull for the red water!"

"As I spoke, the fury of the animal seemed suddenly to die away. He paused in his career, and lay passive on the waves; with his arching back thrown up like the ridge of a mountain. 'The old sog's lying to!' I cried, exultingly. 'Spring, boys! spring now, and we have him! All my clothes, tobacco, every thing I've got, shall be yours, only lay me 'longside that whale before another boat comes up! My grimky! what a hump! Only look at the irons in his back! No, don't look — PULL! Now, boys, if you care about seeing your sweethearts and wives in old Nantuck! — if you love Yankee-land — if you love me — pull ahead, won't ye? Now then, to the thwarts! Lay back, my boys! I feel ye, my hearties! Give her the touch. Only five seas off! Not five seas off! One minute — half a minute more! Softly — no noise. Softly with your oars! That will do —'

"And as the words were uttered, I raised the harpoon above my head, took a rapid but no less certain aim, and sent it, hissing, deep into his thick white side!

"'Stern all! for your lives!' I shouted; for at that instant the steel quivered in his body, the wounded leviathan plunged his head beneath the surface, and whirling around with great velocity, smote the sea violently, with fin and fluke, in a convulsion of rage and pain.

"Our little boat flew dancing back from the seething vortex around him, just in season to escape being overwhelmed or crushed. He now started to run. For a short time, the line rasped, smoking, through the chocks. A few turns round the loggerhead then secured it; and with oars a-peak, and bows tilted to the sea, we went leaping onward in the wake of the tethered monster. Vain were all his struggles to break from our hold. The strands were too strong, the barbed iron too deeply fleshed, to give way. So that whether he essayed to dive or breach, or dash madly forward, the frantic creature still felt that he was held in check. At one moment, in impotent rage, he reared his immense blunt head, covered with barnacles, high above the surge, while his jaws fell together with a crash that almost made me shiver; then the upper outline of his vast form was dimly seen, gliding amidst showers of sparkling spray; while streaks of crimson on the white surf that boiled in his track, told that the shaft had been driven home.

"By this time, the whole 'school' was about us; and spouts from a hundred spiracles, with a roar that almost deafened us, were raining on every side; while in the midst of a vast surface of chafing sea, might be seen the black shapes of the rampant herd, tossing and plunging, like a legion of maddened demons. The second and third mates were in the very centre of this appalling commotion.

"At length, Dick began to lessen his impetuous speed. 'Now, my boys,' cried I, 'haul me on; wet the line, you second oars-man, as it comes in. Haul away, ship-mates! — why the devil don't you haul? Leeward side — leeward! I tell you! Don't you know how to approach a whale?'

"The boat brought fairly up upon his broadside as I spoke, and I gave him the lance just under the shoulder blade. At this moment, just as the boat's head was laid off; and I was straitening for a second lunge, my lance, which I had 'boned' in the first, a piercing cry from the boat-steerer drew my attention quickly aft, and I saw the waist-boat, or more properly a fragment of it, falling through the air, and underneath, the dusky forms of the struggling crew, grasping at the oars, or clinging to portions of the wreck; while a pair of flukes, descending in the midst of the confusion, fully accounted for the catastrophe. The boat had been struck and shattered by a whale!

"'Good heaven!' I exclaimed, with impatience, and in a tone which I fear showed me rather mortified at the interruption, than touched with proper feeling for the sufferers; 'good heavens — hadn't they sense enough to keep out of the red water! And I must lose this glorious prize, through their infernal stupidity!' This was the first outbreak of my selfishness.

"'But we must not see them drown, boys,' I added, upon the instant; 'cut the line!' The order had barely passed my lips, when I caught sight of the captain, who had seen the accident from the quarter deck, bearing down with oar and sail to the rescue.

"'Hold on!' I thundered, just as the knife's edge touched the line; "for the glory of old Nantuck, hold on! The captain will pick them up, and Mocha Dick will be ours, after all!'

"This affair occurred in half the interval I have occupied in the relation. In the mean time, with the exception of a slight shudder, which once or twice shook his ponderous frame, Dick lay perfectly quiet upon the water. But suddenly, as though goaded into exertion by some fiercer pang, he started from his lethargy with apparently augmented power. Making a leap toward the boat, he darted perpendicularly downward, hurling the after oarsman, who was helmsman at the time, ten feet over the quarter, as he struck the long steering-oar in his descent. The unfortunate seaman fell, with his head forward, just upon the flukes of the whale, as he vanished, and was drawn down by suction of the closing waters, as if he had been a feather. After being carried to a great depth, as we inferred from the time he remained below the surface, he came up, panting and exhausted, and was dragged on board, amidst the hearty congratulations of his comrades.

"By this time two hundred fathoms of line had been carried spinning through the chocks, with an impetus that gave back in steam the water cast upon it. Still the gigantic creature bored his way downward, with undiminished speed. Coil after coil went over, and was swallowed up. There remained but three flakes in the tub!

"'Cut!' I shouted; 'cut quick, or he'll take us down!' But as I spoke, the hissing line flew with trebled velocity through the smoking wood, jerking the knife he was in the act of applying to the heated strands out of the hand of the boat-steerer. The boat rose on end, and her bows were buried in an instant; a hurried ejaculation, at once shriek and prayer, rose to the lips of the bravest when, unexpected mercy! the whizzing cord lost its tension, and our light bark, half filled with water, fell heavily back on her keel. A tear was in every eye, and I believe every heart bounded with gratitude, at this unlooked-for deliverance.

"Overpowered by his wounds, and exhausted by his exertions and the enormous pressure of the water above him, the immense creature was compelled to turn once more upward, for a fresh supply of air, And upward he came, indeed; shooting twenty feet of his gigantic length above the waves, by the impulse of his ascent. He was not disposed to be idle. Hardly had we succeeded in bailing out our swamping boat, when he again darted away, as it seemed to me with renewed energy. For a quarter of a mile, we parted the opposing waters as though they had offered no more resistance than air. Our game then abruptly brought to, and lay as if paralyzed, his massy frame quivering and twitching, as if under the influence of galvanism. I gave the word to haul on; and seizing a boat-spade, as we came near him, drove it twice into his small; no doubt partially disabling him by the vigor and certainty of the blows. Wheeling furiously around, he answered this salutation, by making a desperate dash at the

29

boat's quarter. We were so near him, that to escape the shock of his onset, by any practicable manoeuvre, was out of the question. But at the critical moment, when we expected to be crushed by the collision, his powers seemed to give way. The fatal lance had reached the seat of life. His strength failed him in mid career, and sinking quietly beneath our keel, grazing it as he wallowed along, he rose again a few rods from us, on the side opposite that where he went down.

"'Lay around, my boys, and let us set on him!' I cried, for I saw his spirit was broken at last. But the lance and spade were needless now. The work was done. The dying animal was struggling in a whirlpool of bloody foam, and the ocean far around was tinted with crimson. 'Stern all!' I shouted, as he commenced running impetuously in a circle, beating the water alternately with his head and flukes, and smiting his teeth ferociously into their sockets, with a crashing sound, in the strong spasms of dissolution. 'Stern all I or we shall be stove!'

"As I gave the command, a stream of black, clotted gore rose in a thick spout above the expiring brute, and fell in a shower around, bedewing, or rather drenching us, with a spray of blood.

"'There's the flag!' I exclaimed; 'there! thick as tar! Stern! every soul of ye! He's going in his flurry!' And the monster, under the convulsive influence of his final paroxysm, flung his huge tail into the air, and then, for the space of a minute, thrashed the waters on either side of him with quick and powerful blows; the sound of the concussions resembling that of the rapid discharge of artillery. He then turned slowly and heavily on his side, and lay a dead mass upon the sea through which he had so long ranged a conqueror.

"'He's fin-up at last!' I screamed, at the very top of my voice. 'Hurrah! hurrah! hurrah!' And snatching off my cap, I

30

sent it spinning aloft, jumping at the same time from thwart to thwart, like a madman.

"We now drew alongside our floating spoil; and I seriously question if the brave commodore who first, and so nobly, broke the charm of British invincibility, by the capture of the Guerriere, felt a warmer rush of delight, as he beheld our national flag waving over the British ensign, in assurance of his victory, than I did, as I leaped upon the quarter deck of Dick's back, planted my waif-pole in the midst, and saw the little canvass flag, that tells so important and satisfactory a tale to the whaleman, fluttering above my hard-earned prize.

"The captain and second mate, each of whom had been fortunate enough to kill his fish, soon after pulled up, and congratulated me on my capture. From them I learned the particulars of the third mate's disaster. He had fastened, and his fish was sounding, when another whale suddenly rose, almost directly beneath the boat, and with a single blow of his small, absolutely cut it in twain, flinging the bows, and those who occupied that portion of the frail fabric, far into the air. Rendered insensible, or immediately killed by the shock, two of the crew sank without a struggle, while a third, unable in his confusion to disengage himself from the flakes of the tow-line, with which he had become entangled, was, together with the fragment to which the warp was attached, borne down by the harpooned whale, and was seen no more! The rest, some of them severely bruised, were saved from drowning by the timely assistance of the captain.

"To get the harness on Dick, was the work of an instant; and as the ship, taking every advantage of a light breeze which had sprung up within the last hour, had stood after us, and was now but a few rods distant, we were soon under her stern. The other fish, both of which were heavy fellows, lay

31

floating near; and the tackle being affixed to one of them without delay, all hands were soon busily engaged in cutting in. Mocha Dick was the longest whale I ever looked upon. He measured more than seventy feet from his noddle to the tips of his flukes, and yielded one hundred barrels of clear oil, with a proportionate quantity of 'head-matter'. It may emphatically be said that 'the scars of his old wounds were near his new', for not less than twenty harpoons did we draw from his back; the rusted mementos of many a desperate rencounter."

The mate was silent. His yarn was reeled off. His story was told; and with far better tact than is exhibited by many a modern orator, he had the modesty and discretion to stop with its termination. In response, a glass of "o-be-joyful" went merrily round; and this tribute having been paid to courtesy, the vanquisher of Mocha Dick was unanimously called upon for a song. Too sensible and too good-natured to wait for a second solicitation, when he had the power to oblige, he took a "long pull" and a strong, at the grog as an appropriate over-ture to the occasion, and then, in a deep, sonorous tone, gave us the following professional ballad, accompanied by a superannuated hand-organ, which constituted the musical portion of the cabin furniture:

I.
"Don't bother my head about catching of seals!
To me there's more glory in catching of eels;
Give me a tight ship, and under snug sail,
And I ask for no more, 'long side the sperm whale,
   In the Indian Ocean,
   Or Pacific Ocean,
   No matter what ocean;
   Pull ahead, yo heave O!

II.
"When our anchor's a-peak, sweethearts and wives
Yield a warm drop at parting, breathe a prayer for our lives;
With hearts full of promise, they kiss off the tear

From the eye that grows rarely dim — never with fear!
>Then for the ocean, boys,
>The billow's commotion, boys,
>That's our devotion, boys,
>Pull ahead, yo heave O!

III.

"Soon we hear the glad cry of 'Town O! — there she blows!'
Slow as night, my brave fellows, to leeward she goes:
Hard up! square the yards! then steady, lads, so!
Cries the captain, 'My maiden lance soon shall she know!'
>Now we get near, boys,
>In with the gear, boys,
>Swing the cranes clear, boys;
>Pull ahead, yo heave O!

IV.

"Our boat's in the water, each man at his oar
Bends strong to the sea, while his bark bounds before,
As the fish of all sizes, still flouncing and blowing,
With fluke and broad fin, scorn the best of hard rowing:
>Hang to the oar, boys,
>Another stroke more, boys;
>Now line the oar, boys;
>Pull ahead, yo heave O!

V.

"Then rises long Tom, who never knew fear;
Cries the captain, 'Now nail her, my bold harpooner!'
He speeds home his lance, then exclaims, 'I am fast!'
While blood, in a torrent, leaps high as the mast:
>Starn! starn! hurry, hurry, boys!
>She's gone in her flurry, boys,
>She'll soon be in 'gurry', boys!
>Pull ahead, yo heave O!

VI.

"Then give me a whaleman, wherever he be,
Who fears not a fish that can swim the salt sea;
Then give me a tight ship, and under snug sail,
And last lay me 'side of the noble sperm whale;
>In the Indian ocean,

Or Pacific ocean,
Not matter what ocean
Pull ahead, yo heave O!"

The song "died away into an echo", and we all confessed
ourselves delighted with it — save and except the gallant knight
of the seal-club. He indeed allowed the lay and the music to
be well enough, considering the subject; but added: "If you
want to hear genuine, heart-stirring harmony, you must lis-
ten to a rookery of fur seal. For many an hour, on the rocks
round Cape Horn, have I sat thus, listening to these gentry,
as they clustered on the shelving cliffs above me; the surf
beating at my feet, while—"

"Come, come, my old fellow!" exclaimed the captain, in-
terrupting the loquacious sealer; "you forget the evening you
are to have at Santa Maria. It is three o'clock in the morning,
and more." Bidding farewell to our social and generous en-
tertainers, we were soon safely on board our ship, when we
immediately made all sail to the north.

To me, the evening had been one of singular enjoyment.
Doubtless the particulars of the tale were in some degree
highly colored, from the desire of the narrator to present his
calling in a prominent light, and especially one that should
eclipse the occupation of sealing. But making every allow-
ance for what, after all, may be considered a natural embel-
lishment, the facts presented may be regarded as a fair speci-
men of the adventures which constitute so great a portion of
the romance of a whaler's life; a life which, viewing all the
incidents that seem inevitably to grow out of the enterprise
peculiar to it, can be said to have no parallel. Yet vast as the
field is, occupied by this class of our resolute seamen, how
little can we claim to know of the particulars of a whaleman's
existence! That our whale ships leave port, and usually return, in the course of three years, with full cargoes, to swell
the fund of national wealth, is nearly the sum of our knowl-
edge concerning them. Could we comprehend, at a glance,

the mighty surface of the Indian or Pacific seas, what a picture would open upon us of unparalleled industry and daring enterprise! What scenes of toil along the coast of Japan, up the straits of Mozambique, where the dangers of the storm, impending as they may be, are less regarded than the privations and sufferings attendant upon exclusion from all intercourse with the shore! Sail onward, and extend your view around New-Holland, to the coast of Guinea; to the eastern and western shores of Africa; to the Cape of Good Hope; and south, to the waters that lash the cliffs of Kergulan's Land, and you are ever upon the whaling-ground of the American seaman. Yet onward, to the vast expanse of the two Pacifics, with their countless summer isles, and your course is still over the common arena and highway of our whalers. The varied records of the commercial world can furnish no precedent, can present no comparison, to the intrepidity, skill, and fortitude, which seem the peculiar prerogatives of this branch of our marine. These characteristics are not the growth of forced exertion; they are incompatible with it. They are the natural result of the ardor of a free people; of a spirit of fearless independence, generated by free institutions. Under such institutions alone, can the human mind attain its fullest expansion, in the various departments of science, and the multiform pursuits of busy life.

Made in the USA
Middletown, DE
15 April 2016